Brands We Know

Target

By Sara Green

Bellwether Media • Minneapolis, MN

Jump into the cockpit and
take flight with Pilot books.
Your journey will take you on
high-energy adventures as you
learn about all that is wild,
weird, fascinating, and fun!

This edition first published in 2016 by Bellwether Media, Inc.

No part of this publication may be reproduced in whole or in part
without written permission of the publisher.
For information regarding permission, write to Bellwether Media, Inc.,
Attention: Permissions Department,
5357 Penn Avenue South, Minneapolis, MN 55419.

Library of Congress Cataloging-in-Publication Data

Green, Sara, 1964-
  Target / by Sara Green.
      pages cm. -- (Pilot: Brands We Know)
  Summary: "Engaging images accompany information about Target
Corporation. The combination of high-interest subject matter and
narrative text is intended for students in grades 3 through 7"-- Provided
by publisher.
  Audience: Ages 7-12
  Audience: Grades 3 to 7
  Includes bibliographical references and index.
  ISBN 978-1-62617-289-0 (hardcover: alk. paper)
  1. Department stores--Minnesota--History--Juvenile literature. 2.
Stores, Retail--Minnesota--History--Juvenile literature. I. Title.
  HF5465.U64T375 2016
  381'.1410973--dc23
                    2015010412

Printed in the United States of America, North Mankato, MN.

Table of Contents

What Is Target?

A family drives into the parking lot of a **big-box** store. Its red bull's-eye **logo** means it is a Target! Today, the family is shopping for groceries and clothes. They also need sporting goods and pet supplies. Target sells this **merchandise** and much more. The family is sure to find everything they need.

Target is a **chain** of **discount** stores run by the Target Corporation. Its company **headquarters** is in Minneapolis, Minnesota. Today, Target is one of the largest **retail** chains in the United States. The bull's-eye logo is famous around the country. Target sells a wide variety of everyday and seasonal items. Many Targets feature a **pharmacy**, coffee shop, and other services. Target is known for quality products, affordable prices, and friendly service. It makes one-stop shopping easy and fun!

By the Numbers

worth more than
$53 billion
in 2015

#48
on *Fortune* magazine's list
of World's Most Admired
Companies in 2015

nearly
1,800
stores in the
United States

around
347,000
employees

49
states with
Target stores

more than
230
Target stores
in California

The Dayton Family

Target's history began with George Draper Dayton. In 1902, he built a six-story building in Minneapolis, Minnesota. It was home to a **dry goods** store. George changed the name of his store twice. He finally settled on The Dayton Company. It was also known as Dayton's department store. George was an honest and

George Draper Dayton

generous man. His customers knew they would find quality goods and friendly service at his store.

By the 1920s, Dayton's had become a multi-million dollar business. George's sons helped him run the company. After George's death in 1938, one son took over. Later, George's grandsons became the owners. They found new ways to expand the family business. In 1956, the company built Southdale Center in a Minneapolis **suburb**. This was the first indoor shopping mall in the United States. Southdale included a Dayton's department store as one of its **anchors**. The mall was a huge success. In time, the Dayton Company built three more shopping malls in Minnesota. Dayton's was an anchor in each one.

Design for All
2000s–2010s tagline

Southdale, 1956

A Giving Family

The Dayton family has a history of generosity. In 1946, the family began giving away a portion of Dayton's profits. This yearly donation went to the community. This has added up to millions of dollars over time.

During this time, discount stores were becoming more popular. However, many had low-quality merchandise. George's grandsons saw a great opportunity. They decided to build a better discount chain. It would sell high-quality goods at low prices. Dayton employees suggested the Target name and the bull's-eye logo for the new store. In 1962, George's grandsons achieved their dream. They opened the first Target in Roseville, Minnesota. Soon, three more opened in other Minnesota cities. Target was on its way!

In 1969, Dayton's joined with another company called The J.L. Hudson Company. They became Dayton-Hudson. Company **divisions** included Dayton's and Target. It also included other department stores. Soon, Target expanded into cities across the country. Its clean look and friendly service delighted customers. Target quickly started making the most money of any Dayton-Hudson business. By 1979, Target was making $1 billion in yearly sales. The discount chain was a hit!

As Target grew, the chain looked for better ways to serve people. In 1990, a larger store called Target Greatland opened. It offered more merchandise and services such as restaurants and pharmacies. However, Greatlands were eventually replaced by SuperTargets. The first of these opened in 1995. It was the largest Target store. SuperTargets carry a full selection of groceries, including fresh produce and bakery items. Some include new services such as banks.

Clever **advertising** helped Target gain a fun, trendy image. Some ads show household items being used in creative ways. Others make these everyday things seem fashionable. Many popular ads star Target's **mascot** dog, Bullseye. This white bull terrier is also a favorite guest at many Target events. Bullseye sports a bright red collar. The Target logo is painted around one eye. People delight in seeing this famous dog!

Target's popularity led to a major change in the company. Target was Dayton-Hudson's biggest earner. The name had become well known across the country. For these reasons, the company renamed itself Target Corporation in 2000.

Bullseye

**Eat Well.
Pay Less.**
2000s–2010s tagline

What Makes Target Special?

Target has stayed true to the Dayton family's vision. Customers, called "guests," are the chain's main focus. Target's goal is to give guests a pleasant shopping experience. Team members provide helpful, friendly service. Stores are bright, clean, and well-organized. High-quality merchandise is displayed in attractive ways. Wide aisles make pushing a cart easier. Stores also do not disturb guests with music or loudspeaker announcements. To keep up with trends, Target regularly updates its merchandise. Guests enjoy discovering what new items are for sale or in stock.

Target Cartwheel app

Pizza Hut Express

Target Optical

Starbucks

Target Pharmacy

Guests also enjoy Target's extra services. They get **prescriptions** filled at Target Pharmacy. Target **Optical** offers eye exams and glasses. Guests can buy coffee and snacks at Starbucks, Pizza Hut Express, or other in-store restaurants. Target also has **apps**. They help people find stores and get coupons. One even pinpoints an item's exact location in a store.

Over time, Target created its own **brands**. These are less expensive than similar brand-name products. Many have become customer favorites. Thousands of grocery items bear the Archer Farms or Market Pantry brands. Target's up & up brand offers hundreds of items. It includes household, baby, and personal care products. Target also has its own clothing brands, such as Xhilaration and Cherokee. Many Target products are made in ways that protect the environment. Its Simply Balanced brand features fish from **sustainable** sources. Room Essentials furniture is made with wood from sustainable forests. Guests know they can trust the quality of Target's own brands.

Target is also known for its designer collections. These allow guests to buy clothes created by Missoni, Phillp Lim, and other popular fashion designers. Nate Berkus and Lilly Pulitzer designed home decoration lines. Target guests love buying high-end merchandise at discount prices!

Target Brands

Brand Name	Brand Focus
Archer Farms	High-quality foods
Champion	Workout wear
Cherokee	Clothes and shoes for kids
Circo	Clothes, toys, and furniture for kids
Gilligan & O'Malley	Pajamas
Market Pantry	General groceries
Merona	Clothes and accessories for adults
Mossimo	Clothes and accessories for adults
Room Essentials	Furniture, kitchenware, and home accessories
Simply Balanced	Natural and organic foods
Threshold	Furniture and home accessories
up & up	Beauty, household, and personal care products
Xhilaration	Clothes and accessories for juniors

Expect More. Pay Less.

1990s–2010s tagline

Going Downtown

Today, Target is able to meet the needs of more guests than ever. In 2012, Target opened its first CityTarget stores. These mid-sized Targets fit well in crowded, **urban** areas. CityTarget sells many of the same products found at Target or SuperTarget. These items come in easy-to-carry sizes. CityTargets do not offer furniture or other large, bulky items.

CityTarget in Chicago, Illinois

**Fast, Fun,
and Friendly**

Target motto

In 2014, Target launched TargetExpress. It is the company's smallest store yet! Despite its compact size, TargetExpress sells many items. Guests can buy groceries, electronics, and sporting goods. They can also find bedding, beauty products, and a pharmacy. These small Targets are perfect for people who do not own cars. Usually guests only buy as much as they can carry. Short checkout lines mean little to no waiting. Target plans to open more CityTargets and TargetExpress stores in cities around the country. These smaller Targets help make downtown shopping quick and easy!

Committed to Communities

Target is committed to giving back to communities. In 1997, Target launched Take Charge of Education. Guests use special Target cards called REDcards to make purchases. Then Target gives some of the money spent to schools. Target also improves school libraries all over the country. It donates books, computers, and other materials. Since 1997, Target has given more than $900 million to schools and libraries across the country. Soon that number will be $1 billion!

Target also encourages its team members to **volunteer**. Many help repair communities hit by natural disasters. Target volunteers also work with their local police departments. They plan activities that help keep their communities safe. Target works to make our everyday shopping and everyday lives a more pleasant experience.

Around for Good

2010s tagline

COOKIES

PLEASE MAKE SURE PLASTIC PAC...

Daily Bread
Food Bank

DESSERT

PLEASE PUT CAKE MIX AND MUFFIN MIX IN THE FLOUR CATERGORY. THANK YOU!

Daily Bread
Food Bank

35

Target House

Target funds Target House in Memphis, Tennessee. Target House is located near a large children's hospital. It provides housing for families of sick children who need long-term medical care.

Target team members volunteering

Target Timeline

1902

George Dayton builds a dry goods store in Minneapolis, Minnesota

1956

Dayton's builds the world's first indoor shopping mall

1911

The Dayton Dry Goods Company is renamed The Dayton Company

1918

George Dayton creates The Dayton Foundation

1938

George Dayton passes away and one of his sons becomes president of the company

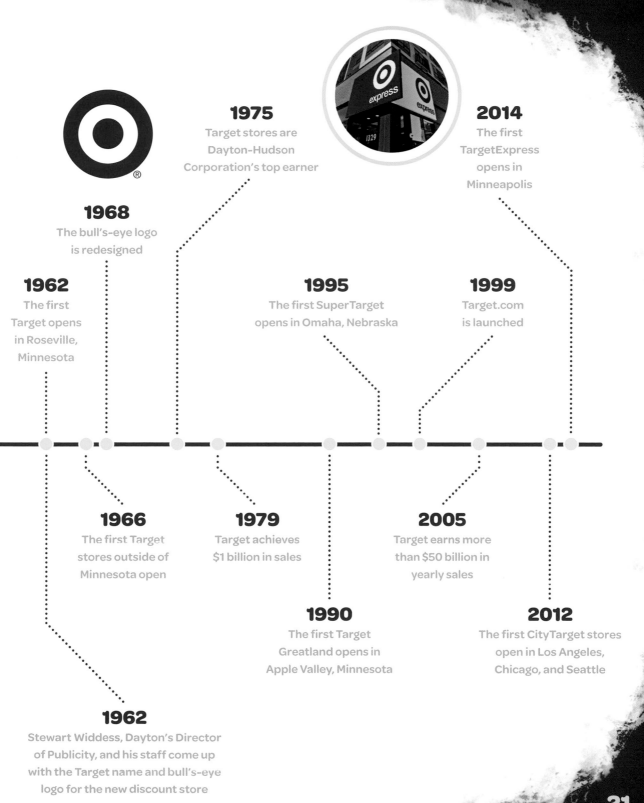

1975
Target stores are
Dayton-Hudson
Corporation's top earner

2014
The first
TargetExpress
opens in
Minneapolis

1968
The bull's-eye logo
is redesigned

1962
The first
Target opens
in Roseville,
Minnesota

1995
The first SuperTarget
opens in Omaha, Nebraska

1999
Target.com
is launched

1966
The first Target
stores outside of
Minnesota open

1979
Target achieves
$1 billion in sales

2005
Target earns more
than $50 billion in
yearly sales

1990
The first Target
Greatland opens in
Apple Valley, Minnesota

2012
The first CityTarget stores
open in Los Angeles,
Chicago, and Seattle

1962
Stewart Widdess, Dayton's Director
of Publicity, and his staff come up
with the Target name and bull's-eye
logo for the new discount store

Glossary

advertising—using notices and messages to announce or promote something

anchors—large department stores located at the ends of shopping malls

apps—small, specialized programs that are downloaded onto smartphones and other mobile devices

big-box—a large, single-story retail store with a rectangular shape

brands—categories of products all made by the same company

chain—a set of related stores or businesses with the same name

discount—selling goods at low prices

divisions—separate parts of a business

dry goods—fabric, thread, clothing, and related items

headquarters—a company's main office

logo—a symbol or design that identifies a brand or product

mascot—an animal or object used as a symbol by a group or company

merchandise—items sold in a store

optical—having to do with the eyes and vision

pharmacy—a place that prepares and gives out medications to people

prescriptions—medications that a doctor officially approves for a person

retail—in the business of selling goods

suburb—a smaller community next to a large city; suburbs usually have more houses than businesses.

sustainable—able to be used without being completely used up or destroyed

urban—relating to cities and city life

volunteer—to do something without expecting money in return

To Learn More

AT THE LIBRARY

Bix, Cynthia Overbeck. *Spending Spree: The History of American Shopping.* Minneapolis, Minn.: Twenty-First Century Books, 2014.

Green, Sara. *Jeff Bezos.* Minneapolis, Minn.: Bellwether Media, 2015.

Mara, Wil. *Sam Walton: Rethinking Retail.* New York, N.Y.: Children's Press, 2014.

ON THE WEB

Learning more about Target is as easy as 1, 2, 3.

1. Go to www.factsurfer.com.

2. Enter "Target" into the search box.

3. Click the "Surf" button and you will see a list of related web sites.

With factsurfer.com, finding more information is just a click away.

Index

The images in this book are reproduced through the courtesy of: MattGush, front cover (shopping cart); dhoffmanimages, front cover (plastic bag); Sheila Fitzgerald, front cover (Archer Farms logo, Market Pantry logo); Bellwether Media, front cover (gift cards, up & up logo, shopping cart symbol), pp. 10, 13 (Pizza Hut Express, Target Optical, Starbucks, iPhone), 16; dcwcreations, front cover (Super Target); Tyler McKay, front cover (Target logo); s_bukley, front cover (dog); Darren Brode, front cover (race car); ryby, front cover (shirt); windu, front cover (pants); Target, Table of Contents (Target logo), pp. 4 (REDcard, reusable bag, iPhone), 13 (Target Pharmacy), 14, 15, 18, 21 (Target logo, Target Express); jimkruger, p. 5; Pakhnyushchy, p. 5 (background); Minnesota Historical Society/ Wikipedia, p. 6; Grey Villet/ Getty Images, pp. 7, 20 (right); Bill Johnson/ Getty Images, p. 8; Dave Buresh/ Getty Images, p. 9; FS2 Wenn Photos/ Newscom, p. 11; Rick Wilking/ Reuters/ Newscom, p. 12; Glen Stubbe/ MCT/ Newscom, p. 17; Vince Talotta/ Getty Images, p. 19; Curt Teich Postcard Archives/ Getty Images, p. 20 (left).